Tuning Into God
SMALL GROUP GUIDE

Eagles: The Very Best of

Geoff Gittli

Standard
PUBLISHING
Bringing The Word to Life

Cincinnati, Ohio

Published by Standard Publishing, Cincinnati, Ohio
www.standardpub.com

Copyright © 2007 by Standard Publishing. All rights reserved. No part of this book may be reproduced in any form, except for brief quotations in reviews, without the written permission of the publisher.

Printed in the United States of America.

Written by: Geoff Gittli
Project editors: Michael Mack and Jim Eichenberger
Cover and interior design: Andrew Quach

All Scripture quotations, unless otherwise indicated, are taken from the HOLY BIBLE, NEW INTERNATIONAL VERSION®. NIV®. Copyright © 1973, 1978, 1984 by International Bible Society. Used by permission of Zondervan. All rights reserved.

Scripture quotations marked (NLT) are taken from the Holy Bible, *New Living Translation*, copyright © 1996. Used by permission of Tyndale House Publishers, Inc., Wheaton, Illinois 60189. All rights reserved.

ISBN 978-0-7847-1997-8

14 13 12 11 10 09 08 07   9 8 7 6 5 4 3 2 1

Tuning Into God:

Table of Contents

Series Introduction	4
Author's Preface	7
Fast Facts about The Eagles	8
1. Take It Easy	9
Releasing Worry • (Matthew 6:25-34)	
2. Desperado	15
Finding Connection • (Romans 8:31-39)	
3. Lyin' Eyes	21
Relationship Wisdom • (Proverbs 2:1-22)	
4. Take It to the Limit	27
Capturing Hope • (John 14:1-7)	
5. Hotel California	33
Trapped by Materialism • (1 Timothy 6:6-11)	
6. Life in the Fast Lane	39
Yielding to God • (Luke 15:11-32)	
The Eagles on the Web	45
Bible Study Web Sites	46
Icebreakers	47

"Music . . . can name the unnameable and communicate the unknowable." —Leonard Bernstein

"Music is a higher revelation than wisdom or philosophy." —Ludwig Van Beethoven

Introducing . . . Tuning Into God!

"Tune your ears to wisdom, and concentrate on understanding" (Proverbs 2:2, *NLT*).

This discussion guide uses a fresh approach to help draw people, regardless of where they are on their spiritual journeys, into a closer relationship with God.

The **Tuning Into God** series is designed to help you and your group:
- develop a deeper understanding of and relationship with God as you look at his Word from brand new perspectives
- be a creative tool to help you reach out to your friends with his message of grace (for instance, in a "seeker" study in your neighborhood or workplace)

The O'Jays' song title, "I Love Music (Any Kind of Music)" says it well! God created each one of us with a musical "soul"! Apparently, God loves music too. Throughout Scripture, we are directed to sing and play music to him. All of his creation—both in Heaven and on earth—is encouraged to "sing for joy" and "burst into song" (Isaiah 44:23). God is even described as our strength and our song (Exodus 15:2; Psalm 118:14; Isaiah 12:2). Music—any kind of music—has the ability to flow into our souls and move us like nothing else can.

Johann Sebastian Bach once said, "The aim and final end of *all* music should be none other than the glory of God and the refreshment of the soul." Even secular music can accomplish that aim. God uses everything in his creation to accomplish his will, even when those things were never intended by their human authors for his purposes (see Isaiah 46:10, 11; Exodus 9:16; Romans 9:17).

⊙ Engaging the Culture

This discussion guide uses popular and spiritually provocative secular songs to engage the culture in which we live. These songs are worldly in nature, so they will, of course, contain worldly words and ideas. Our purpose is not to conform ourselves to these worldly patterns, but to set them next to God's Word to see them for what they are, and then to be transformed by the renewing of our minds (Romans 12:2) as we study and apply Scripture.

Much of secular music is simply a sharing of ideas around some of life's most pressing issues—even around the meaning of life itself. The expression of these ideas through music is much like the Athenians' sharing of the latest ideas in Acts 17. Paul engaged the culture and then interjected God's Word into it. Today, we can also help people who are earnestly seeking to find the "unknown God" they are searching for.

Yes, you will hear some words and ideas you are not used to hearing in a Christian Bible study! But be assured that God's Word deals with these issues and provides the truth to live by.

⊙ How to Use This Guide

All songs used in this guide can be found on *Eagles: The Very Best of* or can be downloaded from a digital music Web site. Each week you will be prompted during the discussion to play the featured song, so have everything ready to listen to the song at that time. Lyrics can be found on numerous Web sites, such as the one listed on page 45 of this book.

Use the selected songs as an entertaining way to launch you into an enlightening study of Scripture. Remember that you'll use this guide not so much to discuss the song, but to dive into God's Word to allow it to transform your mind to God's way of living. If you are the group's leader, be sure to facilitate the discussion so as to spend your time wisely studying God's Word. Gently steer off-track discussions back to what Scripture has to say about the topic.

Each session includes:

The Hook: A light, introductory-style icebreaker that leads the group into the study.

Tune-ology: Brief background material and other interesting information about the song and the author.

Instructions to Play the Song and Lesson Introductory Question: The question simply gets your group to look at the selected song for its overall message and meaning.

Scripture Reading and Discussion: Ask someone from the group to read the Scripture passage and then use the following questions to get the group digging into and talking about the content of the Bible passage. These questions will move the group toward meaning and understanding. While participants on their own may make references to the song, the leader should direct the discussion back to the Bible passage.

The Bridge: A combination of information, a quote, or an interesting fact, along with several questions that tie the Bible passage back to the lyrics of the song. This section also moves the group toward application of the Bible passage.

Tuning In: Application-oriented questions and/or activities that encourage group members to discuss how they will live out the biblical message. This section usually ends with an activity or question that moves group members to formulate an action plan for living out the application during the upcoming week and may include prayer, journaling, additional Bible study, accountability, encouragement, or other practices.

While this discussion guide does not include ideas for worship, prayer, and planning time for outreach and serving, be sure to integrate these important aspects of group life into your meeting.

"Music and rhythm find their way into the secret places of the soul." —Plato

"Music speaks what cannot be expressed, soothes the mind and gives it rest, heals the heart and makes it whole, flows from heaven to the soul." —Unknown

○ Author's Preface

Growing up in the '70s, I often went to sleep with the radio on, listening to the thought-provoking songs of Glenn Frey and Don Henley. The mental images that the songs created would keep me thinking about their meanings and how they applied to my life at the time. Little did I know that the songs of the Eagles were even deeper than I could imagine at that stage of my life!

Frey and Henley met at the Troubadour, where they hoped to be discovered. Instead, they discovered each other out of desperation. At that time, Henley was singing and drumming for a band called Shiloh. Frey had finally got David Geffen to listen to his material. Geffen, manager for Joni Mitchell and Crosby, Stills, Nash & Young, liked his work and suggested he join a band before he started recording. Linda Ronstadt hired him for her band, and they needed a drummer for her upcoming record. Frey asked Henley to join the band, and the rest is history. Most of the Eagles songs are an outcome of their collaborations.

The Eagles' unique and powerful images have meanings that lurk below the surface. My hope is that this discussion guide will help you use these great songs to dive deeper into Scripture and apply God's Word to your life. It is a creative approach to learning about some of the greatest songs ever written and to apply God's Word from a fresh perspective. Dive in and have fun learning!

—Geoff Gittli

Fast Facts about The Eagles

- Drummer Don Henley, guitarist Glenn Frey, bluegrass instrumentalist Bernie Leadon, and bassist and high-harmony singer Randy Meisner toured together in 1971 as members of Linda Ronstadt's band.

- In March of 1972 the Eagles recorded their self-titled debut album with producer-engineer Glyn Johns in London. Glyn Johns had previously produced projects for The Beatles, Led Zeppelin, The Rolling Stones, and The Who.

- On January 1, 1974, guitarist Don Felder joined the Eagles to record their third album, *Already Gone*.

- Veteran rock guitarist Joe Walsh replaced Bernie Leadon in January of 1976.

- The group's first best-of collection, *Their Greatest Hits 1971-1975*, is the best-selling album of all time in the U.S., having sold 29 million copies.

- Randy Meisner left the band in September of 1976 and was replaced by Timothy Schmit, his old band mate from the group Poco.

- In the summer of 1980 Glenn Frey called Don Henley to announce his intention to disband the Eagles. The breakup was not congenial. *Eagles Live* (released in November 1980 to fulfill contractual obligations to the record label) listed five attorneys in the liner notes and the simple statement, "Thank you and goodnight."

- An Eagles tribute album, *Common Thread: The Songs of the Eagles*, was the Country Music Association's Album of the Year in 1993. The project included the work of country music's hottest stars, such as Travis Tritt, Diamond Rio, Suzy Bogguss, and Tanya Tucker among others.

- The Eagles were inducted into the Rock and Roll Hall of Fame in 1998.

"Take It Easy"
Releasing Worry • Matthew 6:25-34

The Hook

1. People seem to find it hard to relax in our society today.

   • Why do you think that is?

   • Share some of your favorite ways to unwind:

Jackson Browne wrote "Take It Easy" for his first album, but he didn't know how to finish the song. He gave it to Glenn Frey, who needed songs for his new band, the Eagles. This was the first song on their first album. Long before it was ever recorded, the Eagles played this song in a club in Colorado, where they played four sets nightly.

Jackson Browne later recorded the song as the lead track on his second album, *For Everyman* (1973). Several other artists, including Billy Mize, Johnny Rivers, and Travis Tritt, have released versions of it.

The song inspired the town of Winslow in northwest Arizona to create "Standin' on the Corner Park". The park is located in downtown Winslow on Route 66.

Tuning Into God

Play the song, "Take It Easy"
(Disc One, Track 1, on *Eagles: The Very Best of*).

As you listen, try to recall what year "Take it Easy" was released. Let the song help you recall some memories of what was happening in your life at the time. (If you were too young to remember or weren't born yet, recall memories you have about the time period when you first remember hearing this song.)

2. What do you think is the main point of this song? What key lines of advice does the singer give?

3. How did you apply some of this advice after you first heard the song?

Read Matthew 6:25-34.

4. Note some central themes of this passage. Explain what is meant by the rhetorical questions found in these verses:

   • v. 25

   • vv. 26, 28

   • v. 27

5. What is Jesus teaching about priorities?

   • Explain a major difference between the priorities of Christians and non-Christians and why that is so (vv. 31, 32).

   • How does being a follower of Jesus affect a person's view of the meaning of life? (v. 33).

   • Some might call a Christian a *Pollyanna,* a person who is foolishly or blindly optimistic, for not worrying about his or her personal needs. Explain why that is *not* a fair description of what the Bible teaches (v. 34).

Tuning Into God

The Bridge

Before their rise to fame, the Eagles were opening on tours for Jethro Tull, Joe Cocker, and Yes. "Take it Easy" (1972) was the first single for the band and it got some airplay, but "it didn't particularly feel successful," recalls Randy Meisner. Glenn Frey concurred: "We realized we weren't the Beatles—it wasn't mass hysteria. Then we cooled out!"

Frey said the message of "Take It Easy" was, "You shouldn't get too big too fast." In the beginning, none of the Eagles seemed comfortable with the idea that they were becoming a success so quickly.

In the end, some would handle success better than others. A particularly jarring scandal involved Don Henley. On the night of November 21, 1980, Henley was arrested for cocaine, Quaalude, and marijuana possession after a 16-year-old prostitute had drug-related seizures in a hotel room. He was charged with contributing to the delinquency of a minor.

6. Critique some of the advice found in "Take It Easy" by comparing and contrasting it to what Jesus said in Matthew 6:25-34:

- Don't let the busyness of life make you go mad.

- Lighten up rather than take life too seriously.

- Stand firm in your beliefs.

- Seek salvation in personal relationships, no matter how fleeting.

Tuning In

7. Summarize the main commands of our study text.

   - How does our society today follow or not follow the principles from this Scripture?

   - How about Christians? How well do you think we follow these principles?

8. How do you feel about where you are compared to where you want to be in life?

9. How can you lighten up while you still can (instead of worrying)?

10. In what specific ways can you find a place to make a stand in life?

11. List three big ideas that you think God wants you to take away from your study of Matthew 6:25-34:

12. Set a goal this week for conquering your worries and fears. Try doing the following:

    • Decide on a particular area in your life in which to conquer worry.

    • Pray each day about not letting worry control your life.

    • When you catch yourself worrying, write down your fears and why you are having them.

    • At the end of the week, evaluate your efforts to conquer that worry.

Session 2

"Desperado"
Finding Connection • Romans 8:31-39

The Hook

1. List some words or phrases that begin with the word *lone*.

   - How are those words or phrases used?
   - What positive images and attributes are associated with the words or phrases?
   - What negative images and attributes are associated with the words or phrases?

2. Tell about the time when you were on your own for the first time.

   - What positive memories do you have of that experience?
   - What negative memories do you have of that experience?

TUNE-OLOGY

Don Henley began writing parts of "Desperado" in the late '60s, but it wasn't arranged until Glenn Frey came along. It was the first of many songs Henley and Frey wrote together. The song has the feel of the American Old West, but was recorded in London.

The song was featured in an episode of *Seinfeld* where Elaine went out with a guy who wouldn't let her speak when the song was playing. "Desperado" has been covered by Linda Ronstadt, Kenny Rogers, The Carpenters, Bonnie Raitt, and Ringo Starr, among others.

Tuning Into God

Play the song, "Desperado"
(Disc One, Track 4, on *Eagles: The Very Best of*).

The entire *Desperado* album had an Old West theme. It included similarly-themed songs such as "Outlaw Man," "Doolin-Dalton," and "Bittercreek." The project was inspired by The Dalton Gang, a notorious group of outlaws.

3. When you first heard "Desperado," what did you think it was about?

- the Old West—tumbleweeds and ghost towns

- playing poker

- loneliness

- growing old

- discontentment

- other: _____

The stressful life of a rock star is a theme that recurs in the songs of the Eagles. Bon Jovi expressed similar ideas in their 1986 song "Wanted Dead Or Alive."

4. Who do you think is the desperado in the song?

5. When have you ever felt like the stress of life has made you an "outlaw" among your peers?

Read Romans 8:31-39.

In the early church, there were Christians from Jewish backgrounds and Christians from totally pagan backgrounds. Many times the former looked down upon the latter because Jews grew up with a much higher moral standard than did pagans.

Paul argued, however, that even the most righteous people who ever lived still rebelled against God and lived as his enemies. We are *all* desperados, running from the rule of a righteous judge. Furthermore, there is nothing that any person could do to earn divine approval.

Finally in Romans 8, Paul shows how people can stop living the life of a fugitive from God's justice.

6. Look at the rhetorical questions in verses 33, 34a.

   • According to Paul's argument, why should Christians *not* feel like desperate outlaws?

   • Look at the word *interceding* in verse 34. Try to define that word in more "Old West" terms and explain its significance to a desperado.

7. Reread verse 35, noting the list of troubles that people face.

   • Take one or two of them and explain how fallen, sinful human beings try to overcome them.

   • How might they be faced differently when one knows that Jesus is by the side of the one going through them?

Tuning Into God

The Bridge

On the surface "Desperado" is about a cowboy who refuses to fall in love, but it has been taken to have a much wider application. It has come to be an anthem for those on the outskirts of society who are always doing battle with the powers that be.

In 2004, Linda Ronstadt sparked controversy during a performance at the Aladdin Casino in Las Vegas. Before singing "Desperado," she dedicated the song to filmmaker Michael Moore. Moore had just released *Fahrenheit 9/11*, a film that sharply criticized the way President Bush handled the September 11, 2001, terrorist attacks on the United States. Ronstadt praised Moore as a patriot who was trying to keep the truth from being covered up. The casino's president was incensed and made the singer leave the stage.

8. Take another look at the song.

- Note some words and phrases in the song that point out some of the problems of living the lifestyle of a desperado.

- What might the apostle Paul have said to the character in the song?

- How would it change the meaning of this song if you capitalized the word *somebody* in the last line?

Tuning In

When we think of the story of the outlaw in the Old West, we think of a man always on the run from the sheriff who wants to arrest and punish him. In contrast, the message of Paul and of the Bible as a whole is that God seeks out those who have rebelled against him not to punish, but to save.

9. Read the following verses. For each verse, explain how the Bible turns the story of the fugitive outlaw upside down.

    - Psalm 119:76

    - Matthew 18:12-14

    - Luke 19:10

    - John 3:16, 17

10. Think of some people you know (including yourself) who live the life of a fugitive from God's justice.

    - How do such people "ride fences" to avoid submitting to the love of God? What are some of those figurative fences?

    - How does that lifestyle take away the highs and lows of life, making life ultimately bland and boring?

    - How does living the life of a desperado imprison people and make freedom an illusion?

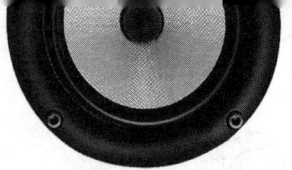

11. Try developing an action plan for connecting more closely to God and his people and for helping other desperados you know to do the same.

- I have been running from God rather than to him in this area of my life:

  _____.

  I resolve to turn that area over to God as a matter of daily prayer.

- I have enjoyed the feeling of being a "lone ranger" in life, but have found that I need others. I will connect more closely with God's people by taking part in this activity that I normally avoid:

  _____

- I have avoided some people who I now realize need to connect with me and with the God I represent. Over the next month I will make a greater effort to befriend the following five people:

  _____

  _____

  _____

  _____

  _____

"Lyin' Eyes"

Relationship Wisdom • Proverbs 2:1-22

The Hook

1. Who was your first boyfriend or girlfriend in school? What's the story?

2. Why do you believe that relationship did not last?

"Lyin' Eyes" helped solidify the reputation of Don Henley and Glenn Frey as songwriters. It was released as the second single from the *One of These Nights* project, and it reached #2 on the *Billboard Hot 100* chart. Furthermore, it received a Grammy Award for Best Pop Performance by a group.

"Lyin' Eyes" has been covered by musicians as diverse as Moe Bandy, Diamond Rio, Peter Calo, and Ray Conniff. In 1980, it appeared on the soundtrack of the John Travolta film, *Urban Cowboy*.

Tuning Into God

Play the song, "Lyin' Eyes"
(Disc One, Track 13, on *Eagles: The Very Best of*).

3. "Lyin' Eyes" tells a story. As you listen, try to picture the main characters. What do they look like? What actor or actress might play each role were the song to be cast as a movie?

4. Describe the lives of each of the characters in this short story using words or phrases from the song. Identify what they might be looking for in their relationships.

- the wife
    - descriptive words or phrases
    - motives

- the husband
    - descriptive words or phrases
    - motives

- the lover
    - descriptive words or phrases
    - motives

Read Proverbs 2:1-22.

5. Sometimes we think of learning as a rather passive pursuit. This passage seems to express a very different idea.

    - What *active* verbs and verb phrases did Solomon use in verses 1-5 to describe how wisdom is obtained?

6. When we ask someone the purpose of learning, they might answer, "To make us smart." Focus on verses 6-11. Explain why there are much greater purposes for gaining wisdom than making us seem intelligent.

7. Review verses 12-20.

    - How often does the word *path* appear?

    - Why do you think this word is used? In what way is it descriptive of human relationships?

    - How does living by God's wisdom change the path of a person's life?

The Bridge

In their biography, the Eagles described their inspiration for this song. As a struggling band in the early days, they noticed a lot of beautiful women around Hollywood who were married to older, wealthy men. One night at a bar, they saw a stunning young women being followed, several steps behind, by an overweight, older, rich man. One of the Eagles commented, "Look at her. She can't even hide those lyin' eyes." The rest of the band scrambled for cocktail napkins to write down lyrics to go with his observation.

8. There are three lies in this song: the woman lies to her husband, to her boyfriend, and to herself.

    - How would you summarize each of the three lies?

    - How could following the principles of this Scripture have prevented some of the conflict described in the song?

9. How could wisdom have guarded the path of:

    - the rich old man?

    - the boyfriend?

    - the woman herself?

10. How, specifically, could the characters in this song have kept on the "paths of the righteous" (v. 20; also see v. 9)? What difference would it have made?

Tuning In

Some speculate that Solomon wrote the book of Proverbs as a training manual for young men going into royal service. During the reign of Solomon both the temple and royal palace were built. The wars of David that had stabilized the territory of Israel had led to the time of peace and prosperity in Solomon's reign. More and more people were living in Jerusalem and other cities, so young leaders who had practical answers about life in this type of society were a necessity.

Thinking back to "Desperado," "Lyin' Eyes" presents an irony. In the former, the title character was told to establish loving relationships to solve his problems. In the latter, the main character *did* establish relationships, but her new life did not bring lasting change. The missing ingredient, it seems, is godly wisdom.

11. When someone becomes a Christian, he or she begins living a "new life" (Romans 6:3, 4; Colossians 3:1-11). In 2 Corinthians 5:17, the apostle Paul tells us, "Therefore, if anyone is in Christ, he is a new creation; the old has gone, the new has come!"

    • How does this new life change things?

    • In what ways has your new life not changed things—you're still the same old person you used to be?

12. Rate your own relationship wisdom by placing yourself on the appropriate place on each of these line graphs:

   • I aggressively pursue godly wisdom in my life.

   rarely true   always true

   What I will do to improve my rating:

   • My godly wisdom protects me from unnecessary hurt in my relationships.

   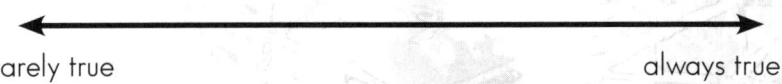

   rarely true   always true

   What I will do to improve my rating:

   • My godly wisdom directs me to make good relationship decisions.

   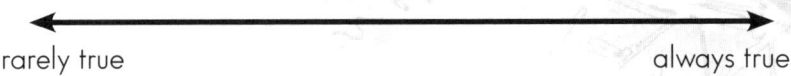

   rarely true   always true

   What I will do to improve my rating:

Session 4

"Take It to the Limit"
Capturing Hope • John 14:1-7

The Hook

1. When you are all alone at the end of the day, on what hopes and dreams do you reflect?

2. Tell about a time when you achieved something you hoped for but were disappointed in the end.

TUNE-OLOGY

"Take It to the Limit" was written by Don Henley, Randy Meisner, and Glenn Frey. Randy Meisner sang lead. After the song's huge success, Meisner decided to go out on his own. He quickly fell into obscurity, and the Eagles continued to become legends. This is the only Eagles single on which Meisner sang lead.

"Take It to the Limit" was the third single released from the album, *One of These Nights*. It was released on November 15, 1975, and went to #4 on the U.S. *Billboard Hot 100*. It was also the Eagles' greatest success to that point in the U.K., with the single going to #12 on the charts. "Take It to the Limit" was covered by country musicians Willie Nelson and Waylon Jennings as the title track of their duet album, *Take It to the Limit*, which was released in 1983.

Play the song, "Take It to the Limit"
(Disc One, Track 15, on *Eagles: The Very Best of*).

Meisner usually sang high harmonies rather than lead as he did in this song. In fact, after he left the band, Frey sang this lead in concerts, but in a much lower key. As you listen to the song, pay close attention to the mood created by the lilting rhythms and soaring vocals.

3. What words come to mind when describing the feelings evoked by the song?

4. What are some of your favorite lines or phrases in this song? Why?

Read John 14:1-7.

5. This familiar passage is a part of Jesus' address to his disciples at the last supper. He knew it would be the last time he would address all of his disciples before his crucifixion.

   - What point is Jesus trying to make to Thomas and the other disciples at this time?

   - Why do you think that the disciples had so much trouble understanding him at this point?

   - We often hear these words read at funerals. Some have suggested, however, that the place Jesus was making for his disciples in the Father's house does not refer as much to afterlife as it does the church. See Ephesians 2:19; 1 Timothy 3:15; Hebrews 10:21; 1 Peter 2:5. How do those verses change your view of Jesus' words?

6. Biblical faith is consistently referred to as a way, a walk, a road, a path, etc. Explain what these verses say in that regard:

   - John 14:5, 6

   - Psalm 119:105

   - Jeremiah 31:21

   - John 10:7-9

The Bridge

Randy Meisner got his start with the band Poco, playing the infamous Troubadour nightclub. After many fights in the studio, Meisner quit the group. Rick Nelson found out he had left Poco and asked Randy to join his new group, the Stone Canyon Band. Meisner played on several albums but left before they hit the charts with "Garden Party." Meisner met Glenn Frey and Don Henley, who invited him to join the band that would become the Eagles. Meisner then left the Eagles after "Take It to the Limit" became a big hit.

"Take It to the Limit" tells the story of a person chasing after things in life but never seeming to get what he hopes for. He is looking for signs and for people to believe in him, but he is never getting that satisfaction. He just keeps coming back and running back for more and more of the same. Meisner, like the character in this song, seemed always to be chasing success without understanding it was right in front of him.

An interesting contrast can be seen in the life of a bandmate of Meisner from Poco. Richie Furay had success with Steven Stills in the '60s band, Buffalo Springfield, and later founded Poco. Though successful in the music world, Furay never found satisfaction until peddle steel guitar player Al Perkins led him to faith in Jesus. Furay became a follower of Christ and has been the senior minister of Calvary Chapel in Broomfield, Colorado, for more than twenty years.

7. Imagine that you are Richie Furay and you run into your old friend Randy Meisner. Referring only to John 14:1-7 and the words to "Take It to the Limit," explain to your friend how he can find the hope he seeks.

Tuning In

8. Think of people you know that remind you of Meisner and the character in this song.

    - What big questions do they have about life?

    - Where do they look for the answers?

9. Consider your own hopes and dreams.

    - How have the dreams and plans for your life changed from when you were younger?

    - When you decided on the dreams you would pursue, did you ask God his plan for your life? If so, how? If not, why not?

    - How can you change how you think about the future?

    - What percentage of your thoughts about your future concern life here on earth and what percentage concern your eternal future in Heaven? How do you think these percentages need to be adjusted, if at all?

10. Which of these road signs best describes your life right now?

- **Detour**—Things keep distracting me from what is truly important.

- **Under Construction**—A lot needs to be done in my life before God can use me.

- **Watch Out for Falling Rocks**—I always seem to be waiting for the next disaster to occur in my life.

- **Children at Play**—Family concerns seem to hinder my walk with God.

- **Other**—_____

What steps will you take to change your sign?

Session 5

"Hotel California"
Trapped by Materialism • 1 Timothy 6:6-11

The Hook

1. Tell about a time when you were literally trapped. Were you in a locked room, tangled up in something, or in another confining situation? Tell how it happened and how you felt.

2. Tell about a time when you were figuratively trapped. What ensnared you? How did this happen and how did you feel?

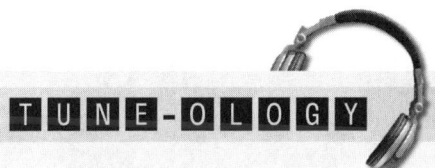

TUNE-OLOGY

Don Felder got the ball rolling on this song. He had the chord progressions and took it to Don Henley and Glenn Frey. They put the words down, and Joe Walsh wrote all the guitar parts and arranged everything. The song was recorded at three different sessions until the Eagles got the version they wanted. The biggest problem was finding the right key for Henley's vocal.

The *Hotel California* album is #37 on the *Rolling Stone* list of the 500 greatest albums of all time. The Eagles spent eight months in the studio, polishing take after take. Don Henley said, "We locked ourselves in. We had a refrigerator, a ping-pong table, roller skates, and a couple of cots. We would go in and stay for two or three days at a time. We were in search of the perfect note song."

Play the song, "Hotel California"
(Disc One, Track 17, on *Eagles: The Very Best of*).

3. "Hotel California" is arguably one of the best classic rock songs ever written. What thoughts and feelings surface when you hear this song?

4. Over the years, many interpretations and rumors have been associated with this song. What have you heard the lyrics of this song are about and why?

- Drug use

- Suicide

- A ghost story

- A nightmare

- Robotic/technological takeover of earth

- Satanism

- Alien abduction

- Materialism and excess in LA

- Visiting a brothel

- Nothing: Just a great song

- Other: _____

Read 1 Timothy 6:6-11.

5. Notice the phrase "godliness with contentment" in verse 6. Try to give an example of:

   - godliness with contentment

   - godliness *without* contentment

   - *godlessness* with contentment

   - godlessness *without* contentment

6. What are some specific ways that greed and the pursuit of excess affect one's ability to achieve happiness?

7. Notice that the "love of money," not money itself, leads to evil (v. 10). Notice that Paul quickly adds in verses 17-19 that wealth can be used for God's glory.

   - Paraphrase those verses.

   - Give an example of how wealth has been used to "take hold of life that is truly life."

The Bridge

Glenn Frey was asked about the meaning of "Hotel California." He responded, "That record explores the underbelly of success, the darker side of Paradise, which is sort of what we were experiencing in Los Angeles at that time. So that just became the metaphor for the whole world and for everything you know. We just decided to make it Hotel California, . . . a microcosm of everything going on around us."

8. Note the plays on words concerning a famous jewelry store and a luxury car in the second verse of the song.

   • Explain what you think is meant by that line.

   • Judging from his words to Timothy, how do you think the apostle Paul would respond to that line if he lived today?

Frey once compared "Hotel California" to an episode of classic TV's *The Twilight Zone*. The song seems to jump from one scene to the next and doesn't necessarily make sense.

9. Consider Frey's assessment. How does that mood add to the message of the song? In what ways does living a life of excess cause similar disorientation?

Tuning In

10. Paul warned that "People who want to get rich fall into temptation and a trap" (1 Timothy 6:9). The last verse of "Hotel California" seems to echo that idea.

    - Contrast what the Bible and the song say about the possibility of escape from that trap of materialism.

    - How do you account for that difference?

11. Create a plan for escaping the trap of materialism by summarizing these verses

    - 1 Timothy 6:7, 8

    - 1 Timothy 6:11

    - Proverbs 11:24, 25

    - Proverbs 19:17

12. God wants your heart to be in the right place. See Matthew 6:19-24.

    - Where do you think your heart is when it comes to money, power, and materialism?

    - What do you need to do first to be sure your heart is aligned with God's desire for you?

13. Take out any bills you have in your wallet or purse. Attach a self-stick note to several of these and on each one write one or two of the phrases from 1 Timothy 6:6-11 that are particularly meaningful to you. As you spend this money in the coming days:

- Take time to read the words on the bill.

- Take a moment to ask God to keep you from loving your possessions.

- Ask God to help you use your wealth not to purchase contentment, but to "pursue righteousness, godliness, faith, love, endurance and gentleness" (1 Timothy 6:11).

- Whenever you place additional bills in your wallet, notice the words "In God We Trust" on the back of each. Ask God to continue to teach you what that means when it comes to possessions.

Session 6

○ "Life in the Fast Lane"
Yielding to God • Luke 15:11-32

The Hook

1. What's the fastest you ever traveled? What's the story—why, when, and how did this happen?

2. When have you been lost on a car trip? How did you get lost? How did you find your way to where you were going?

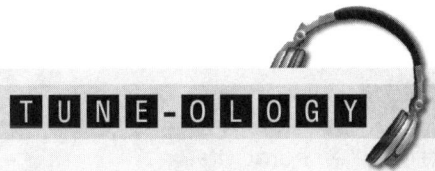

TUNE-OLOGY

The song would be a part of the soundtrack for the film comedy *FM* (1978). This music-rich movie about a radio station demonstrated how influential the Eagles were in the '70s. The flick's soundtrack is filled with friends and alumni of the band including Steely Dan, Linda Ronstadt, Randy Meisner, and a solo effort by Walsh.

Ringo Starr recorded a memorable cover of "Life in the Fast Lane" several years later.

Play the song, "Life in the Fast Lane"
(Disc Two, Track 1, on *Eagles: The Very Best of*).

"Life in the Fast Lane" was the third single released from *Hotel California* and became another huge hit for the band. The stinging guitar riff announced that Joe (formerly of the James Gang) Walsh would shape the future releases of the band. His hard-rock sound significantly moved the Eagles from their country-rock roots.

3. As you listen, pay attention to the feelings the song evokes in you.

   • What musical aspects are particularly jarring to you?

   • What words or phrases do you find disturbing?

   • Do these help you better understand the song or do you just find them distracting? Explain.

4. How are the characters described?

   • What words and phrases describe the characters?

   • How might you feel about these characters if they were acquaintances you had to be around regularly?

   • Speculate on the story of these characters and summarize it briefly.

Read Luke 15:11-32.

5. Consider the characteristics of the man we usually refer to as the "prodigal son" from verses 11-20a.

   • What do you think was driving him to leave his home and embark on this new life?

   • What excesses became a part of his life?

   • What do you think was going on inside him when he realized he had made a mistake?

6. Consider the characteristics of the prodigal's older brother from verses 25-30.

   • How does he respond to the return of his brother?

   • To what extent is that reaction justified? To what extent is it unjustified?

7. Clearly, the father described in verses 20b-24, 31, 32 is a metaphor for God.

   • How is the love of God like that of a human father?

   • How does the love of God differ from that of a human father?

Tuning Into God

The Bridge

The title for this song coined a phrase that has become a part of mainstream language. While some songs inspire catch phrases that last for a short time ("Who Let the Dogs Out?") or that remain tied to a specific genre ("Stand By Your Man"), the phrase "Life in the Fast Lane" has endured and has totally transcended its original context.

8. How would you describe someone who is living life in the fast lane?

- Give an example of how someone misses one of life's stop signs and takes a turn for the worse.

- What types of things tend to pull people into the fast lane?

A couple of different theories exist as to the factual basis for the song. Many argue that the song is about Stevie Nicks and Lindsey Buckingham of the group Fleetwood Mac and the effect a rock star lifestyle had on their relationship. Nicks dated Henley after she broke up with Buckingham. Others believe that it recounts a time when Frey was in the car with a drug dealer traveling down the highway at breakneck speed. Either way, it is clearly a warning about the dangers of living a lifestyle of excess.

9. Look again at Luke 15:11-32.

- How was the life of the prodigal son similar to the characters in this song?

- Imagine that this song *is* about the prodigal son. Try your hand at completing the song by adding a verse describing the resolution of the story.

Tuning In

In a July 2000 newspaper interview with the *Florida Weekly Planet*, Henley said, "We get so accustomed to being addicted to what's going on in the outer world that we completely ignore our inner worlds, our hearts and minds . . . So few of us get a still, quiet moment throughout a day . . . That leads to our basic unhappiness. We can't be still and we can't listen."

10. God wants us to be still and listen to him. (For example, see Psalm 4:4; Psalm 46:10; Isaiah 28:14; Jeremiah 2:4; Matthew 11:15; Revelation 2:11.)

    - What caused the prodigal son to be still and listen to God?

    - What situations may cause people today to do the same?

    - How much time daily would you say you devote to shutting out the outside world and spending time alone with God? How do circumstances in your life affect that practice?

11. Consider how you react to those around you who are living lives of excess.

    - Why do such people disturb or even frighten you?

    - How can you be more aware when such a person has a "pigpen" moment of stillness and is ready to listen?

12. Evaluate yourself this week by comparing and contrasting yourself to each of the main characters in the story. How are you like each? How do you differ? In what ways do you need to change?

- the rebellious prodigal son

    - similarities:

    - differences:

    - necessary changes:

- the judgmental, self-righteous brother

    - similarities:

    - differences:

    - necessary changes:

- the ever-vigilant, ever-loving father

    - similarities:

    - differences:

    - necessary changes:

The Eagles on the Web

Official Web Sites
Band Web site
http://www.eaglesband.com/

The Eagles Official MySpace page
http://profile.myspace.com/index.cfm?fuseaction=user.viewprofile&friendID=16813761

Fan Sites
The Fastlane
http://www.eaglesfans.com/

Tribute Bands
The Alter Eagles
http://www.altereagles.co.uk/

Hotel California
http://www.hotelcal.com/

Lyrics
http://www.mp3lyrics.org/e/eagles/

Purchasing The Eagles: *The Very Best of*
CD
http://www.rhino.com/store/ProductDetail.lasso?Number=73971

Download
http://www.apple.com/itunes/store/music.html

The Eagles Memorabilia
http://www.irocknroll.com/Eagles.html

The Eagles Ringtones
http://www.funtonia.com/ringtones/Eagles/

Sites listing for informational purposes only. Appearance on the list does not constitute an endorsement by Standard Publishing.

Bible Study Web Sites

Bible Text
Search the Bible in over 50 versions and 35 languages
http://www.biblegateway.com/

Online concordance and other handy tools
http://www.blueletterbible.org/

Classic Commentaries
Search more than a dozen commentaries by chapter of the Bible
http://eword.gospelcom.net/comments/

Bible Dictionary
Look up important Bible words and phrases with a simple index
http://bibletools.org/index.cfm/fuseaction/Def.default

Lexicons
Do word studies from the original Hebrew or Greek
http://www.studylight.org/lex/

Bible Study Tools
A variety of tools are found here
http://bible.crosswalk.com/

http://bible.oneplace.com/

Audio Bible
Listen to the Bible in MP3 format
http://heargoodnews.org/Bible/

Cyber Hymnal
Coordinate classic hymns to any study with these searchable indices
http://www.cyberhymnal.org/

Sites listing for informational purposes only. Appearance on the list does not constitute an endorsement by Standard Publishing.

Icebreakers

One of the purposes of a small group Bible study is to get to know one another better. On occasion, you may wish to start a session with one of these games that helps build community in a fun way.

Clusters
At the leader's signal, members need to cluster themselves together according to each of these criteria:
- favorite color
- season of the year in which you were born
- number of siblings
- state in which you were born

The leader will keep the game moving. As soon as one set of clusters is made, he or she will give another criterion to rearrange the group.

I Have Never
The leader should give each group member the same number of "markers" (coins, poker chips, pieces of wrapped candy) as the number of people in the group. Each member, in turn, should make a true statement about himself or herself beginning with the phrase, "I have never." Statements should be about an activity that the member has *not* done, but believes that many others in the group *have* done. For example:
- I have never been to Florida.
- I have never eaten lobster.
- I have never owned a new car.

Each member who *has* done what the speaker has not must give the speaker a marker. Play progresses until all members have had a turn.

Poetic Intros
Each group member is given a few minutes to come up with an introduction of himself or herself that employs a common poetic element. Common examples would include:
- alliteration (Golfing Glenda, Numbers Nick)
- rhyme (Slim Kim, Silly Billy)
- metaphor (Sparks Lewis, Carla the Swan).

Ask members to explain their intros.

Help! I'm a Small Group Leader!

Small Group Help Guides are ideal for any leader who is looking for practical tips to help them begin and lead a small group.

Let's Get Started!
03015 • 9780784720738

Now That's a Good Question!
03038 • 9780784720745

Why Didn't You Warn Me?
03042 • 9780784720752

I'm a Leader . . . Now What?
03050 • 9780784720769

To purchase visit your local Christian bookstore or find it online at www.standardpub.com.

Standard PUBLISHING
Bringing The Word to Life